italian vegetables

italian vegetables

delicious recipes for appetizers and sides

Maxine Clark

photography by Peter Cassidy

RYLAND
PETERS
& SMALL

LONDON NEW YORK

First published in the
United States in 2005
by Ryland Peters & Small, Inc.
519 Broadway, 5th Floor
New York, NY 10012
www.rylandpeters.com

10 9 8 7 6 5 4 3 2

Library of Congress
Cataloging-in-Publication Data

Clark, Maxine.
  Italian vegetables : delicious recipes for
appetizers and sides / Maxine Clark.
    p. cm.
  Includes index.
  ISBN 10: 1-84172-820-9
  ISBN 13: 978-1-84172-820-9

  1. Cookery (Vegetables) 2. Cookery,
Italian. I. Title.
  TX801.C566 2005
  641.6'5'0945--dc22
                        2004016248

Printed in China

Dedication
To Annabel R., a Kiwi in a million!

Acknowledgments

My thanks as always to Elsa, my editor
at RPS for such a lovely commission.
Peter Cassidy takes such care over the
photography—it is beautiful! Coupled with
Róisín's carefully considered propping, the
shots are timeless. Grateful thanks must go
to my trusty assistants in the kitchen,
Belinda Spinney and Lizzie Harris, for their
enthusiasm and hard work through thick
and thin. Steve Painter's patience and good
design is always appreciated—as are his
tasting abilities. Again, thanks to Nowelle
Valentino-Capezza for her help with the
Italian translations.

Senior Designer Steve Painter
Commissioning Editor
    Elsa Petersen-Schepelern
Editor Susan Stuck
Production Patricia Harrington
Art Director Gabriella Le Grazie
Publishing Director Alison Starling

Food Stylist Maxine Clark
Stylist Róisín Nield

Notes
• All spoon measurements are level unless
otherwise specified.
• All eggs are extra-large unless otherwise
specified. Uncooked or partially cooked
eggs should not be served to the very
young, the frail or elderly, those with
compromised immune systems, or to
pregnant women.
• Ovens should be preheated to the
specified temperature. Recipes in this book
were tested in several kinds of oven—all
work slightly differently. I recommend using
an oven thermometer and consulting
the maker's handbook for
special instructions.

contents

vegetables italian-style

Italians have a special way with vegetables, and it's no wonder, when they can choose from such abundance and variety. In Italy, vegetables are eaten when in season, ripe, and at their best—it is this is that makes them so special: they actually taste of something! When cooked, their flavors are not disguised, but enhanced by simple combinations of ingredients; the fewer the better, often mixing sweet, salt, and sour together.

It's interesting that what are thought to be the most typical Italian vegetables are not indigenous. Where would Italian cooking be today without the tomato? This newcomer to Italian cuisine was brought to Europe and Asia from the Americas, along with the potato, eggplant, and pepper.

This book is a celebration of the vegetables grown and used in Italy today. Italians certainly do make the most of the infinite variety and high quality of their vegetables, as anyone can see walking through a street market at almost any time of year.

It is spring that brings the greatest excitement. Asparagus in all its guises floods the market stalls— from spindly wild varieties, to thin green stems flushed with purple, to Italy's beloved white asparagus. This opens the floodgates to baby artichokes, a riot of salad leaves and herbs, new potatoes, fava beans snug in their furry pods, and sweet new peas.

In summer, a riot of salad greens, wild and cultivated, herbs such as basil, parsley, and mint, tomatoes, fennel, traffic-light bell peppers, eggplant, and fresh beans spill onto laden stalls, just begging to be quickly cooked or preserved.

Fall brings the most hallowed edible delights of all, *porcini e tartufi* (wild mushrooms and truffles, black and white). Pumpkins, squash, root vegetables, cauliflowers, and cabbages such as Tuscan cavolo nero, and even horseradish all make an appearance.

Even in winter, there will still be plenty of salad leaves. From the cooler north to the baking south, Italy has climates and soils to suit many varieties.

The Italian way of preparing vegetables is always a celebration of the vegetable itself, bringing out the most in its flavor or texture, for us to marvel at and enjoy. When each vegetable is in season, you will certainly know about it. The more abundant they are, the cheaper they are, and that's when they are bottled and preserved for the winter. These vegetables are picked when perfectly ripe and ready to eat, at the proper time of year. Cooking them in a simple fashion will only enhance them.

shoots and leaves

Asparagus with egg and Parmesan is made all over Italy during the asparagus season. It is a very simple dish requiring the best and freshest ingredients, so try to use real Parmigiano Reggiano, free-range eggs, and firm asparagus. Cook the eggs on the day of serving or the whites will be a bit rubbery and the yolks can start to discolor—even better, cook to order and serve warm. Always keep hard-cooked eggs covered with cold water to exclude the air, even if peeled—this keeps them fresh and retains the color of the yolks. Overboiling eggs will give that characteristic black ring around the yolk—use a kitchen timer.

asparagus with parmesan and chopped eggs

asparagi, uova e parmigiano

4 fresh free-range eggs

1 lb. fresh asparagus

¼ cup extra virgin olive oil

3 oz. piece of fresh Parmesan cheese

sea salt and freshly ground black pepper

Serves 4 as a light appetizer, or as part of an antipasti selection

Cook the eggs in a saucepan of boiling, salted water for about 10 minutes (from boiling), depending on size. Transfer to cold water to cool, then peel when cold. Cut the eggs in half, then finely chop the whites and crumble the yolks. Reserve both.

To trim the asparagus, snap or cut off any woody ends from the stems. Steam for 10–12 minutes until tender and still bright green, depending on the thickness. The tip of a sharp knife should glide easily into the thickest part of the stem when cooked. Drain well and toss with olive oil, salt, and pepper.

Arrange on warm plates, then sprinkle with the chopped egg white and crumbled yolk. Shave the Parmesan over each serving, using a vegetable peeler—and be generous.

This speciality of Genoa in Liguria uses anchovies as a way of adding savory saltiness, just as fish sauce does in Southeast Asian cooking. It doesn't taste overly fishy, but gives the earthy spinach a depth it would not have otherwise. The combination of salt (anchovies) and sweet (dried fruit), coupled with mild, creamy pine nuts in savory dishes is common all over Italy. You can toast the pine nuts in the olive oil if you wish, but it's not usually done in this dish.

spinach with anchovies and pine nuts

spinaci alla genovese

2½ lb. fresh spinach

½ cup good olive oil

4 anchovy fillets in oil, drained and chopped

3 tablespoons chopped fresh flat-leaf parsley

3 tablespoons dried currants or small raisins, soaked in warm water for 15 minutes

¼ cup pine nuts

freshly grated nutmeg

sea salt and freshly ground black pepper

Serves 4

Tear the stems off the spinach, discard the stems, and wash the leaves very well in plenty of cold water to remove any grit and sand. Shake dry in a colander or salad spinner, but leave some water clinging to the leaves.

Put the leaves in a covered saucepan and cook for a few minutes until they wilt. Drain well in a colander but do not squeeze dry— you need large pieces of spinach.

Warm the oil in a large skillet, add the chopped anchovies and parsley, and stir for 2–3 minutes over medium heat until the anchovies dissolve. Add the spinach, drained currants, and pine nuts. Add a good grating of nutmeg, taste, season with salt and pepper to taste, and stir-fry for about 5 minutes until heated through, glossy, and well mixed. Serve immediately.

Fresh young artichokes are wonderful cooked in this simple way. They are easy to prepare, but it is worth wearing light rubber gloves to prevent black fingers. Baby artichokes are quite different from the fat, globe ones. They are slightly smaller than the size of your hand, elongated, purple-green, and usually sold in bunches. They have very immature chokes inside and I never bother removing them.

sautéed artichokes with thyme and cool ricotta

carciofi fritti al timo con ricotta

8–12 medium purple-green artichokes with stems and heads, about 4 inches long

1½ lemons

½ cup good olive oil

1–2 tablespoons chopped fresh thyme

⅔ cup dry white wine

at least 4 oz. fresh ricotta cheese

sea salt and freshly ground black pepper

Serves 4

To prepare the artichokes, fill a large bowl with water and squeeze in the juice of ½ lemon to acidulate it. Use another ½ lemon to rub the cut portions of the artichoke as you work. Snap off the dark outer leaves, starting at the base. Trim the stalk down to about 2 inches. Trim away the dark green outer layer at the base and peel the fibrous outside of the stalk with a vegetable peeler. Cut about ½ inch off the tip of each artichoke. As they are prepared, put the artichokes in the lemony water until needed—this will stop them discoloring. When ready to cook, drain and cut in half lengthwise.

Heat the olive oil in a large skillet until hot, then add the artichokes. Sauté for 3 minutes without moving them, then turn them over and cook for another 2–3 minutes until tender. Transfer to a warm serving dish.

Add the thyme to the pan and cook over high heat for a few seconds to release the aroma. Add the wine and boil hard to reduce by half. Season with a squeeze of lemon juice, salt, and pepper. Crumble the ricotta around the edge of the plate of artichokes and pour the hot thyme sauce on top. Serve immediately.

Fennel bulb takes on a completely different character when cooked slowly. It is soft and creamy with a very mild aniseed flavor more akin to celery. Sweet leeks balance it nicely, and the cream and lemon transform this into a very soothing dish. I like to serve this recipe with summery white fish dishes or chicken with a few extra fennel seeds and lemon zest toasted in olive oil sprinkled on top.

fennel and leeks braised in cream and lemon

finocchi e porri in umido

2 medium fennel bulbs

2 large or 4 medium leeks (about 1½ cups after trimming)

4 tablespoons unsalted butter

1 teaspoon fennel seeds (optional)

finely grated zest and juice of 1 unwaxed lemon

2 tablespoons white wine or dry vermouth

1 cup heavy cream

1 cup milk

freshly grated nutmeg

sea salt and freshly ground black pepper

Serves 4

Trim the stalks, fronds, and root ends from the fennel bulbs. Reserve any tender stalks and fronds and chop them to use for serving. Cut the bulbs into 4–6 wedges. Cook in boiling salted water for 10 minutes, then drain.

Trim the leeks, cut into thick rounds, and rinse in cold water to remove any grit. Melt the butter in a shallow braising pan or deep skillet with a lid. When foaming, add the leeks and sauté over brisk heat for 1 minute. Add the fennel seeds, if using, then the lemon juice, lemon zest, and wine, bring to a boil, and boil hard until reduced by half. Tuck in the fennel so it nestles into the leeks.

Put the cream, milk, and grated nutmeg in a bowl, add salt and pepper to taste, stir well, then pour over the fennel and leeks. Slowly bring to a boil, then turn down the heat, cover, and simmer very gently for about 35 minutes or until the fennel is tender at the thickest part. Serve immediately, sprinkled with any reserved chopped fennel fronds.

Note To cook in the oven, cover the dish with foil and bake for 35–40 minutes at 375°F.

My friend Carla Tomasi created this simple but delicious recipe. She cooks it in a screaming hot wok so the broccoli is slightly charred and caramelized. Fabulous! Turn the kitchen exhaust fan to full blast—you need courage, heat, and smoke. Alternatively, cook it outdoors, as we do in Sicily. For this dish you need a large, wide, cast iron skillet or large wok with lid, able to withstand intense heat.

broccoli rabe
with olives and chiles

broccoletti all'arrabbiata

12 fat unpeeled garlic cloves

9 tablespoons extra virgin olive oil, plus extra if necessary

a spring of thyme or rosemary

4 whole fresh red chiles (long, thin ones)

1½ lb. broccoli rabe, each shoot cut in half lengthwise (keep all the leaves on)

3 oz. dry-cured Greek-style black olives (pitted if you must)

sea salt and freshly ground black pepper

a small, shallow baking pan

aluminum foil

Serves 4–6

To roast the garlic, put the whole, unpeeled cloves in the baking pan, toss with 3 tablespoons of the olive oil, then add the thyme, salt, and pepper. Cover tightly with foil and bake in a preheated oven for 20 minutes at 400°F for about 20 minutes until soft and browned.

Prick the chiles with a knife or they will explode during cooking. Turn the kitchen exhaust fan to high—it won't be on for long. Heat the skillet or wok until smoking hot, pour in the remaining olive oil, and, after a few seconds, add the broccoli. (You may have to cook this in 2 batches if your pan is not big enough—don't overcrowd it.) Watch out for spluttering oil and noise at this stage—cover the pan immediately with the lid, but keep it on the heat. When the noise subsides, take off the lid and stir-fry the broccoli over fierce heat until the edges look charred and the characteristic smell of "burnt" broccoli fills your kitchen.

Transfer to a warm serving dish, leaving some oil behind. Add the chiles to the pan, stir for 1 minute, then add the olives. The chiles will start to pop and the skin will detach from the flesh and turn bright orange. Add to the broccoli with the roasted garlic and toss well, adding salt and pepper to taste. Serve immediately.

⅓ cup dried currants or golden raisins

12 saffron threads or one small package (0.6g) saffron powder

1 medium cauliflower, about 2 lb.

¼ cup olive oil

1 onion, thinly sliced or finely chopped

2 garlic cloves, finely chopped

6 anchovy fillets in oil, rinsed and coarsely chopped,

sea salt and freshly ground black pepper

a handful of fresh basil leaves, to serve

la mollica fritta

¼ cup olive oil

1 whole garlic clove, peeled and lightly bruised to crack open

¼ cup dry or fresh bread crumbs

Serves 4

In Sicily, when it comes to cauliflower, you have choices. Unblanched green cauliflower (*broccolo calabrese*), blanched white cauliflower (*broccolo bianco*), and a curious lime green variety with graphically pointed florets (*broccolo romanesco*)— all can be cooked in the same way. This recipe is based on a wonderful dish, cooked for me by Signora Ravidà, who is originally from Palermo. She uses it to dress pasta, but I like it on its own as a vegetable.

cauliflower with saffron and toasted bread crumbs

broccolo con zafferano e mollica fritta

To make the *mollica fritta*, heat the oil in a skillet, add the garlic clove, sauté gently until lightly brown, then remove it from the pan. Stir in the bread crumbs and cook over medium heat, stirring constantly, for 2 minutes until golden. Immediately, pour into a strainer set over a bowl to drain. Let cool.

Put the currants in a small bowl and pour over boiling water to cover. Let soak for 20 minutes. Put the saffron in a cup, add 3 tablespoons warm water, and leave to infuse for 15–20 minutes. Remove the leaves and tough stalk from the cauliflower and divide the head into large florets. Cook for just 5 minutes in boiling salted water. Drain, reserving ⅔ cup of the cooking water.

Heat the olive oil in a deep skillet and gently sauté the onion and garlic for about 5 minutes until soft and golden. Stir in the anchovies and the drained currants and cook for 3 minutes until the anchovies dissolve. Add the saffron and its water, the drained cauliflower, and the reserved cauliflower water. Stir well, then heat to a slow simmer. Season with pepper only. Partially cover with a lid and cook for 5 minutes until the cauliflower is tender. Serve sprinkled with the *mollica fritta* and a few torn basil leaves.

peas, beans, and lentils

Fresh peas and beans need almost no cooking at all, and this dish makes the most of their freshness. If I have time, I like to use the pea pods to make a quick pea stock to give the dish extra flavor. Add more stock if the dish looks dry—there should be plenty of sweet buttery juices.

peas and green beans with prosciutto

piselli e fagiolini al prosciutto

2 cups shelled fresh green peas (about 1 lb. in the pod)

8 oz. thin green beans

6 oz. thickly sliced prosciutto crudo (such as Parma ham, serrano ham, or even pancetta)

4 tablespoons unsalted butter

1 small onion, finely chopped

Serves 4

If using peas in the pod, shell them and reserve the pods and peas separately. Coarsely chop the pods, put them in a saucepan, barely cover with water, and bring to a boil. Simmer for 10 minutes, then strain and set aside.

Meanwhile, trim the beans and cut them in half. Slice the prosciutto into thin strips. Melt the butter in a medium saucepan, add the onion, and cook gently for 5 minutes until softening but not browning. Add the peas and beans and ½ cup pea stock (or water), with salt and pepper to taste. Stir well, then cover with a lid and simmer for 5 minutes. Uncover and stir in the prosciutto. Cook over moderate heat for a couple of minutes, then serve immediately.

green beans with toasted ground almonds and lemon

fagiolini con mandorle pestate

1 lb. fine green beans, trimmed

about ½ cup extra virgin olive oil

⅓ cup ground almonds (see note below right)

1 garlic clove, crushed

1 tablespoon freshly grated lemon zest

2 tablespoons freshly squeezed lemon juice

3 tablespoons chopped fresh flat-leaf parsley

sea salt and freshly ground black pepper

Serves 4

Bring a saucepan of salted water to a boil and add the beans. Boil for about 6 minutes until tender but crisp.

Meanwhile, heat ¼ cup of the olive oil in a skillet and add the ground almonds and garlic. Toss and stir this mixture over medium heat for a couple of minutes until golden brown—take care not to let them burn. Stir in the lemon zest and set aside.

Drain the beans immediately they are ready, return to the pan, and toss with the remaining 3 tablespoons olive oil, the lemon juice, and salt and pepper to taste. Pile onto a warm dish and sprinkle with the toasted almonds and parsley. Serve immediately.

green beans cooked with onion, tomato, and fennel seeds

fagiolini alla fiorentina

1 lb. fine green beans, trimmed

¼ cup extra virgin olive oil

1 medium onion, thinly sliced

1 teaspoon fennel seeds, lightly crushed

1 tablespoon tomato paste or purée

sea salt and freshly ground black pepper

Serves 4

Bring a saucepan of salted water to a boil and add the beans. Boil for about 6 minutes until tender yet crisp. Meanwhile, heat the olive oil in a skillet and cook the onion for about 5 minutes until just beginning to color and soften. Drain the beans immediately they are ready, then set aside.

Add the crushed fennel seeds to the onion with plenty of salt and pepper. Mix the tomato paste with ⅓ cup warm water and add to the onion mixture. Bring to a boil and stir in the beans, tossing well to coat with the sauce. Taste and season again. Cover and simmer gently for 5 minutes more, then serve.

Note If you have the time, grind your own almonds and the result will be so much better. Put them in the freezer for 30 minutes, then grind them in a food processor using the pulse button. This will prevent them becoming oily.

This exquisite medley of green vegetables from western Sicily is one of the best ways to use sweet garden peas (yes, even frozen ones), fava beans, and artichokes. Fava beans taste much better if popped out of their skins to reveal the bright green tender bean. This is traditionally cooked for quite some time (about 45 minutes), because it used to be made with dried beans, but I have shortened the cooking time to keep the freshness and color of the vegetables. It is often served as a soup, or you can add creamy ricotta to make a light lunch.

sicilian green vegetables

frittedda

2 cups shelled fava beans, fresh or frozen and thawed, (1½ lb. before shelling)

4 tablespoons olive oil

8 oz. scallions, coarsely chopped

4 fresh, canned, or frozen artichoke hearts, quartered

1¼ cups vegetable stock or water

2 cups shelled peas, fresh or frozen and thawed (1 lb. before shelling)

a good pinch of sugar, to taste

2 tablespoons chopped fresh mint

sea salt and freshly ground black pepper

Serves 4

Bring a large saucepan of salted water to a boil, add the fava beans, and boil for 1 minute. Drain and plunge them into a bowl of cold water to cool them quickly and set the color. Nick the skin at the top of a bean and gently squeeze at the bottom to pop it out. Continue until all are done.

Heat the oil, add the scallions, and cook over gentle heat for a couple of minutes until they wilt and soften, but do not let brown. Add the fresh artichokes, if using, then the stock or water. Season well with salt and pepper, bring to a boil, then reduce the heat and simmer for 5 minutes.

Add the peas and cook for a further 5 minutes, then gently stir in the fava beans and canned or preserved artichoke hearts, if using. Simmer for another 3–4 minutes. Remove from the heat, taste, add a good pinch of sugar, then stir in the mint. Let cool so the flavors will develop. Serve at room temperature.

Note To prepare fresh artichokes, see page 13.

Any type of dried bean will work well in this recipe—only the cooking times will differ. To make sure that the onion isn't too strong, soak the slices in cold water for 10 minutes and this will draw out the strong juice. Alternatively, you could blanch them for 1 minute in boiling water, to which a couple of squeezes of lemon juice have been added—this will soften the texture and flavor.

cannellini beans with olive oil and mint

fagioli bianchi in umido con la menta

2½ cups dried white beans, such as cannellini, haricot, or navy beans

2 garlic cloves, unpeeled but smashed open

6–8 whole mint leaves, plus 3 tablespoons chopped or torn mint

⅓ cup extra virgin olive oil

1 small red onion, finely sliced into rings or half moons

sea salt and freshly ground black pepper

Serves 4

Soak the beans overnight in about 8 cups cold water. The next day, drain and put them in a large saucepan. Add the garlic cloves, the whole mint leaves, and pepper. Cover with cold water, slowly bring to a boil, then turn down the heat and simmer for 25–30 minutes until tender. Times will vary according to the freshness of the beans. Drain well and remove the garlic and mint.

Put the olive oil, chopped mint, and onion in a bowl and mix with a fork. Add the drained beans and toss them carefully with the dressing. Taste and check the seasoning—you may have to add salt—and serve warm or at room temperature.

Sensational with grilled food! If you can't be bothered cooking chickpeas, use canned, but heat them before you add the other ingredients so that they absorb all the flavors. If you like, serve the chickpeas with the basil piled high on top to mix in as you eat it. A squeeze of lemon juice is good too.

¾ cup dried chickpeas (garbanzo beans), soaked in cold water overnight or 14 oz. canned chickpeas, drained and rinsed

½ teaspoon baking soda (if using dried chickpeas)

6 fat garlic cloves, lightly smashed with their skins on

6 medium purple-green artichokes with stems, heads about 4 inches long

1½ lemons

¼–⅓ cup extra virgin olive oil

1 medium red onion, finely chopped

1 fresh red chile, seeded and finely chopped

a large pinch of dried oregano

sea salt and freshly ground black pepper

1½ cups fresh basil leaves, coarsely torn or chopped

Serves 6

chickpeas with artichokes, chile, olive oil, and basil

ceci e carciofi ai sapori del sud

If using soaked dried chickpeas, drain and rinse them. Put them in a saucepan, add the baking soda and garlic, and cover with cold water. Bring to a boil and simmer for 30 minutes to 1 hour until tender. Times will vary according to the age of the beans. While the chickpeas are cooking, get everything else ready.

To prepare the fresh artichokes, follow the method on page 13. When ready to cook, drain them and cut in half lengthwise. Heat half the olive oil in a large skillet until hot, then add the artichokes. Cook for 3 minutes without moving them in the pan, then turn them over and cook for another 2–3 minutes until tender.

When the chickpeas are cooked, drain, then remove and discard the garlic. Add the hot chickpeas to the artichokes and their oil, the remaining olive oil, the onion, chile, and oregano, then toss gently. Don't add the basil until the chickpeas have cooled down (basil will turn black if mixed with hot ingredients). Add salt and pepper to taste, then serve at room temperature. Like similar salads, this one is even better the next day.

Note If using canned chickpeas, use only 1 garlic clove, crushed. Add it to the pan after cooking the artichokes. Cook for 1 minute, then add to the remaining ingredients.

A rich, wintry stew of lentils, onions, and herbs—perfect to serve with game dishes, duck, and of course, meaty Italian sausages. Sometimes, it is even better served on its own with a stack of grilled bread, rubbed with garlic and sprinkled with olive oil, as a filling supper dish in front of a crackling log fire. Red wine is the only accompaniment.

lentils braised with little onions and herbs

lenticchie e cipolline in umido

12 small pearl onions

2 tablespoons olive oil

2 oz. cubetti di pancetta (cubed Italian bacon) or lardons

2 carrots, finely chopped

2 celery stalks, finely chopped

3 garlic cloves, finely chopped

3 bay leaves

2–3 sprigs of thyme

a sprig of rosemary

2 cups brown lentils

½ cup light dry red wine

1 tablespoon balsamic vinegar

3 tablespoons chopped fresh flat-leaf parsley

2 tablespoons unsalted butter

sea salt and freshly ground black pepper

Serves 6

To peel the onions, put them in a bowl and cover with boiling water. Leave for 2–3 minutes, then drain. Peel off the loosened skins while they are still warm, leaving the onions whole. Trim the root end, but not completely, because this will hold them together.

Heat the oil in a saucepan or casserole dish and add the pancetta. Let cook slowly for 5 minutes to release the fat, then add the carrots, celery, and garlic. Stir well and cook over medium heat for about 5 minutes until beginning to soften. Add the bay leaves, thyme, rosemary, onions, lentils, wine and vinegar. Cook over high heat for 1 minute, then add enough water to cover everything completely. Season to taste with salt and pepper. Bring to a boil, turn down the heat, cover, and simmer gently for about 40 minutes until the lentils are completely soft and they have absorbed most of the liquid. Remove from the heat, discard the herbs, and stir in the chopped fresh parsley and the butter. Serve immediately.

roots, onions, and mushrooms

Carrots are electric orange in Sicily and taste fantastic. Sicily is also the home of Marsala, which comes in all varieties from bone dry to rich and sweet, and I wish this selection were more widely available outside the home country. The nuttiness of the dry Marsala cooks into the sweet carrots, transforming them into something very special indeed. This old recipe is almost a version of French Vichy Carrots, with olive oil taking the place of the usual butter.

carrots with olive oil and marsala

carote al marsala

1¼ lb. carrots, peeled or scraped if young

3 large garlic cloves, unpeeled

6 tablespoons extra virgin olive oil

1¼ cups dry Marsala (or ½ cup dry sherry mixed with ¾ cup sweet Marsala)

sea salt and freshly ground black pepper

2 tablespoons chopped fresh flat-leaf parsley, to serve

Serves 6

Slice the carrots into thin rounds or sticks. Rinse well and pat dry. Crush the garlic cloves to open them up, but don't crush to a pulp. Heat the oil in a heavy skillet until just warm, add the garlic, and sauté gently for 5 minutes until lightly golden. This will flavor the oil without too much harsh garlic taste. Remove and discard the garlic.

Add the carrots and cook over medium heat for 2–3 minutes, tossing them around occasionally. Pour in the Marsala, bring to a boil, then turn down to a simmer, cover, and cook until the carrots are tender (about 10 minutes, depending on thickness). By this time, the Marsala will have emulsified with the olive oil to make a thin sauce—if there seems to be too much, lift out the carrots and boil the sauce hard to reduce. Taste and season with salt and pepper. Transfer to a serving dish, top with the parsley, and serve.

The natural sugars in the vegetables are used in this Neapolitan dish to caramelize and combine with the vinegar to give its characteristic flavor. It is normally done quickly in a skillet, but when cooking in quantity, I have had great success roasting them in the oven.

sweet and sour carrots and zucchini with mint

carote e zucchini "a scapece"

2 medium zucchini

2 medium carrots

⅓ cup extra virgin olive oil

2 tablespoons wine vinegar

a few sprigs of mint, plus extra to serve

sea salt and freshly ground black pepper

Serves 4

Trim the zucchini and carrots and cut into matchsticks the size of your little finger. Put half the olive oil in a bowl, add the carrots, and toss to coat. Transfer the carrots to a roasting pan and cook in a preheated oven at 400°F for 15 minutes.

Meanwhile, toss the zucchini in the remaining olive oil, then stir into the carrots when they have cooked for 15 minutes. Roast together for a further 10 minutes until tender and caramelized. Remove from the oven, season with salt and pepper, then add the mint and vinegar to the roasting pan, mixing well.

Set the pan over high heat on top of the stove and let it bubble for a few seconds to reduce the vinegar. Mix well. Serve hot or at room temperature with extra mint.

Potatoes simply cooked in milk is a classic dish and this is my variation. The milk is enriched with mascarpone and scented with bay leaves instead of nutmeg, giving it a "greener" flavor. Waxy potatoes are best for this dish and are commonly used throughout Italy.

potatoes baked with bay leaves and mascarpone

patate al latte, mascarpone e alloro

4 fresh bay leaves, or more to taste

1 lb. waxy yellow-fleshed potatoes, such as Yukon Gold, peeled and thinly sliced

6 oz. mascarpone cheese

1 scant cup milk

sea salt and freshly ground black pepper

an ovenproof dish, buttered

Serves 4

Put 2 bay leaves in the buttered ovenproof dish. Arrange the potatoes in the dish in layers. Put the mascarpone and milk in a saucepan and season well with salt and pepper. Add the remaining bay leaves and slowly bring to a boil, beating gently to help dissolve any lumps of mascarpone. Pour the hot milk mixture over the potatoes and tuck in the bay leaves. For a stronger flavor, tuck bay leaves around the edge of the dish, as in the photograph.

Bake in a preheated oven at 350°F for about 1¼ hours or until the potatoes are tender when pierced with the tip of a sharp knife. The potatoes will not absorb all the liquid.

A treat for potato and chile lovers, this dish is simplicity itself, but it is important to use a good olive oil, because it is very much a part of the dish. I use large new potatoes, which have an almost creamy texture and absorb the olive oil well. However, you can use any potatoes—it will work with almost anything. Personally, I don't peel the potatoes as they do in Italy: if the skins are thin, there's no need.

the devil's potatoes

patate alla diavola

1 lb. large new potatoes, unpeeled

2 fresh red chiles

1 cup fruity olive oil

sea salt and freshly ground black pepper

aluminum foil

Serves 4

Boil the potatoes whole in a large saucepan of salted water.

While they are boiling, cut the chiles in half lengthwise, remove the seeds, and chop the flesh finely (wear rubber gloves to protect your fingers if you like). Heat the olive oil very gently in a small skillet and add the chiles—they should delicately fizzle when added. Stir briefly, then remove from the heat. Add salt and pepper to taste.

When the potatoes are cooked, drain, then when cool enough to handle, slice thickly and arrange half the slices in a single layer on a dish. Pour half the chile oil over the potatoes, then top with the remaining potatoes and pour over the remaining oil. Cover with aluminum foil and let stand for 10 minutes before serving with a little extra salt and pepper. They should be served warm.

In the Middle Ages, Venice was one of the world's great trading nations, bringing spices and other goods and foods from all over the known world. This dish is redolent with medieval Venetian flavors such as cinnamon. Serve it with rich, fatty dishes, such as roast duck, lamb, or pork.

sweet and sour onions and leeks

cipolle e porri in saor

8 oz. whole pearl onions

8 oz. thick leeks

¼ cup extra virgin olive oil

1 large garlic clove, finely chopped

1 celery stalk, finely sliced

2 tablespoons currants, soaked in warm water for 20 minutes

2 tablespoons chopped fresh flat-leaf parsley

2 tablespoons tomato purée or 1 tablespoon tomato paste

a pinch of cinnamon

1 cup red wine vinegar

¼ cup grappa or brandy

3 tablespoons sugar

sea salt and freshly ground black pepper

Serves 4

To peel the onions, put them in a bowl and cover with boiling water. Leave for 2–3 minutes, then drain. Peel off the loosened skins while they are still warm, leaving the onions whole. Trim the root end, but not completely, as this will hold them together. Trim the leeks and cut into 1-inch lengths.

Bring a large saucepan of salted water to the boil, add the onions, boil for 6 minutes, then lift them out with a slotted spoon and set aside. Add the leeks to the boiling water and parboil them for 4 minutes. Drain well in a colander.

Heat the oil in a large skillet, add the garlic, celery, drained currants, and parsley, and cook for 2–3 minutes but do not let brown. Add the onions and leeks and cook gently for 2 minutes.

Put the tomato purée, cinnamon, vinegar, grappa, and sugar in a small bowl and mix well. Pour into the onions and leeks, bring to a boil, and boil hard for 1 minute. Add 1 cup water, return to a boil, then simmer partially covered with a lid for 15–20 minutes until the onions and leeks are cooked through but still quite firm and the sauce thick and syrupy. Serve immediately or at room temperature.

Farro is an ancient form of wheat that is often used in Italy to make soups, salads, and even desserts. You can find it in gourmet stores, or under the name "wheat berries" or "wheat grain" in natural food stores. It is delicious and chewy and makes a wonderful earthy salad combined with sweet beets and warm dressing. Barley makes a good substitute. The salad should be served warm.

1½ cups farro (or wheat berries), soaked in cold water for 2 hours

1 small onion, halved

1 carrot, peeled and halved

1 celery stalk, halved

1 bay leaf

2 whole garlic cloves, lightly crushed but kept whole

⅔ cup extra virgin olive oil

4 oz. pancetta (Italian bacon), cut into matchsticks

1 lb. small cooked beets, peeled and quartered

1 fat garlic clove, finely chopped

3 tablespoons red wine vinegar

½ teaspoon sugar

6 scallions, white and green parts chopped

a large bunch of arugula, about 10 oz., torn if the leaves are large

sea salt and freshly ground black pepper

Serves 4

beet, wheat, and arugula salad

insalata di barbabietole, farro e rucola

Drain the soaked farro and put in a large saucepan with the onion, carrot, celery, bay leaf, and garlic cloves. Add water to cover. Bring to a boil, turn down the heat, and simmer for about 45 minutes or until tender and firm but not falling apart and mushy. Drain, then remove and discard the vegetables.

Heat 2 tablespoons of the olive oil in a skillet and cook the pancetta until golden and crisp. Remove the pancetta and drain on paper towels. Return the pan to the heat and add the beets. Sauté for 2–3 minutes, then add to the bowl of pancetta.

Add the chopped garlic to the hot pan and sauté until just browning. Immediately deglaze the pan with the red wine vinegar and add the sugar, boiling until it has dissolved. Pour in the remaining olive oil, stir well, and heat gently but do not boil. Add salt and pepper to taste. Put the farro, pancetta, beets, scallions, and arugula in a large bowl and mix gently. Pour in the dressing and toss lightly but thoroughly. Serve immediately before it becomes soggy.

Mushroom *polpette* are delicious on their own, or served as a snack with drinks. If using cultivated mushrooms, add a shake or two of wild mushroom powder (I use Shake O'Cini by L'Aquila) to make them taste like wild mushrooms—I find this invaluable for adding a wild mushroom accent to recipes.

wild mushroom patties

polpette di funghi di bosco

1 lb. mushrooms such as portobello, big flat mushrooms, or wild porcini

½ cup olive oil

3 garlic cloves, finely chopped

3 tablespoons chopped fresh flat-leaf parsley

¼ cup freshly grated pecorino cheese

2 eggs, beaten

¼–⅓ cup fresh bread crumbs

sea salt and freshly ground black pepper

lemon wedges, to serve

Serves 4

Chop the mushrooms finely. Heat ¼ cup of the olive oil in a skillet, add the mushrooms and garlic, and sauté for about 5 minutes or until all the moisture has been driven off. Spread out on a metal tray to cool.

When cold, scrape the mixture into a bowl and beat in the parsley, pecorino, eggs, and ¼ cup of the bread crumbs. If the mixture is too sloppy to shape into balls, add the remaining bread crumbs. Taste and season well with salt and pepper.

Using dampened hands, shape into 16 balls or *polpette* and slightly flatten them. Arrange on a tray lined with plastic wrap, cover with more plastic wrap, and refrigerate until ready to cook.

Heat the remaining oil in a skillet and sauté the *polpette* on each side until golden brown and firm. Drain on paper towels, season with salt, and serve immediately with lemon wedges.

Someone once said that life is too short to stuff a mushroom: wrong! The light stuffing in this recipe complements the mushroom's rich meaty flavor. If using a cultivated type, add a shake of wild mushroom powder (see page 45) to the caps before you add the stuffing.

6 large mushroom caps, such as portobello, flat open mushrooms, or porcini, approximately 1 lb.

2 tablespoons olive oil, plus extra for brushing

2 garlic cloves, finely chopped

3 tablespoons chopped fresh flat-leaf parsley

½ cup black olives, pitted and chopped

3 sun-dried tomatoes, sliced

a pinch of ground hot red pepper

8 oz. fresh ricotta cheese

sea salt and freshly ground black pepper

3 tablespoons freshly grated Parmesan or pecorino cheese, to serve

a baking sheet, oiled

Serves 6

ricotta-stuffed mushrooms
funghi farciti

Pull the stalks off the mushrooms and chop the stalks finely. Heat the oil in a skillet and add the chopped stalks, garlic, parsley, and olives and sauté for a couple of minutes to soften the garlic. Remove from the heat and transfer to a bowl. Stir in the tomatoes, hot red pepper, salt, and pepper, then stir in the ricotta very briefly—it must not be smooth.

Brush the mushroom caps all over with olive oil and arrange open-side up on the baking sheet. Spoon the filling into the mushrooms in loose mounds. Sprinkle with the grated cheese and bake in a preheated oven at 375°F for 15–20 minutes or until the tops are pale golden. Serve immediately.

tomatoes, eggplant, and bell peppers

Funghetto has nothing to do with mushrooms as the name in Italian might suggest. It refers to a method of cooking involving a lot of hot oil. Sautéing cubed eggplant concentrates the flavor and creates a lovely brown crust on the sides, so don't shy away from it. A good tip is to soak the cubed eggplant in heavily salted water instead of sprinkling with salt then rinsing. It is less messy, and I think works better than the traditional method—just remember to dry the eggplant very well before cooking.

golden eggplant with tomatoes and capers

melanzane al funghetto

2 medium eggplant, about 1 lb.

3 tablespoons salt

sunflower or olive oil, for cooking

2 tablespoons tomato purée or sun-dried tomato purée, or 1 tablespoon tomato paste

1 tablespoon small capers in vinegar, drained

3 tablespoons chopped fresh flat-leaf parsley

2 garlic cloves, very finely chopped

sea salt and freshly ground black pepper

Serves 4

Trim the eggplant and cut into bite-size cubes, about ¾ inch square. Half fill a large bowl with cold water and stir in the salt until dissolved. Add the eggplant and put a plate on top to hold them under the water. Set aside for 30 minutes, then remove the plate and drain through a colander. Rinse under cold water, then dry very well on a clean dish towel or with paper towels.

Pour ½ inch depth of oil into a wok or large skillet. Heat until a piece of bread will instantly sizzle when it hits the oil. Cook the eggplant in batches until deep golden brown, then drain on paper towels.

Dilute the tomato purée with ¼ cup water and add the capers. Pour into a large skillet, bring to a boil, add the eggplant, and toss well to coat with the tomato. Add salt and pepper to taste. Mix the parsley and garlic together in a small bowl. Pile the eggplant into a warm dish, sprinkle with the parsley and garlic mixture, and serve hot or warm.

Very simple, this dish relies on pan-grilling the eggplant perfectly. There is nothing worse than an undercooked eggplant, so make sure you baste with plenty of oil, and don't let the pan get too hot or the eggplant will burn before they brown—they should gently sizzle. Add a little crushed or chopped garlic to the dressing if you like, but the mint and lemon flavors are quite delicate.

2 medium eggplant (about 14 oz.)

regular olive oil, for basting

dressing

½ cup extra virgin olive oil

finely grated zest and juice of 1 ripe unwaxed lemon

2 tablespoons balsamic vinegar

1–2 teaspoons sugar

¼ cup very coarsely chopped fresh mint

sea salt and freshly ground black pepper

a stove-top grill pan or outdoor grill

Serves 4

pan-grilled eggplant with lemon, mint, and balsamic dressing

melanzane alla griglia con salsa di menta

To make the dressing, put the oil, lemon juice and zest, and balsamic vinegar in a bowl and beat well. Add the sugar, salt, and pepper to taste—it should be fairly sweet. Stir in half the mint, then set aside.

Heat a ridged stove-top grill pan until hot or light an outdoor grill and wait for the coals to turn white. Cut each eggplant into 8 thin slices, brush lightly with olive oil, add to the pan or grill, and cook for 2–3 minutes on each side until golden brown and lightly charred. Arrange the slices on a large platter and spoon the dressing over the top. Cover and set aside so that the eggplant absorb the flavors of the dressing. Sprinkle with the remaining chopped mint and serve.

Transform even the dullest supermarket tomato into a Mediterranean delight! Packing tomatoes together tightly in a single layer will make sure they don't dry out during the long cooking needed to concentrate their flavor. Although the delicate lactic flavor of *mozzarella di bufala* is best in salads, it would be lost here, so use balls of regular mozzarella. (The rectangular blocks are better for pizza toppings.)

baked tomatoes with basil and melting mozzarella

fonduta di pomodori

12 medium tomatoes, about 2 lb.

good olive oil

1 cup fresh basil leaves, finely sliced

8 oz. mozzarella cheese, cubed

sea salt and freshly ground black pepper

a baking dish, about 8 x 10 inches, lightly oiled

Serves 4

Cut the tomatoes in half around their "equators" and arrange them cut side up in the baking dish. Make sure they are packed together tightly in a single layer, because they should collapse into a solid layer of gooey tomato when cooked.

Sprinkle with salt, plenty of pepper, and lots of olive oil. Bake in a preheated oven at 350°F for about 1 hour. If they have not collapsed and concentrated by this time, cook for longer. When cooked, remove from the oven, put the basil on the tomatoes, then spread the mozzarella on top of the basil. Return to the cooling oven for 2 minutes to help the mozzarella melt—on no account should it brown, just melt into creamy pools. Serve immediately.

These bell peppers are a vegetable and pasta course in one. They should be luscious and soft, with a wrinkled browned exterior. The garlicky cherry tomatoes keep the pasta moist, and the chile and pecorino give a hint of sharpness. A delicious antipasto and also a good accompaniment for fish.

roast bell peppers stuffed with pasta and tomatoes

peperoni ripieni

4 medium yellow or red bell peppers

2 oz. capelli d'angelo or very fine spaghetti

⅓ cup extra virgin olive oil

12 ripe cherry tomatoes, quartered

2 garlic cloves, finely chopped

¼ cup chopped fresh basil

½ cup pine nuts, coarsely chopped

½ teaspoon dried hot red pepper flakes (optional)

1 cup freshly grated pecorino cheese

sea salt and freshly ground black pepper

a baking dish, lightly oiled

Serves 4

Slice the tops off the bell peppers and reserve. Scrape out and discard all the seeds and white pith. Set the peppers upright in a lightly oiled dish small enough to fit them snugly. If they don't stand upright, shave a little piece off the base, but not right through.

Cook the pasta in plenty of boiling salted water until just *al dente*, about 8 minutes or according to the package instructions. Drain well and toss with 2 tablespoons of the olive oil.

Put the tomatoes in a bowl with another 2 tablespoons of oil, the garlic, basil, pine nuts, pepper flakes, and pecorino and mix well. Add the pasta to the peppers, filling them by two-thirds, then spoon in the tomato mixture. Put the pepper lids on top and brush liberally all over with the remaining olive oil. Bake in a preheated oven at 425°F for 25–30 minutes or until the peppers start to wrinkle and blister. Serve hot or at room temperature.

My favourite recipe for sweet peppers is this one from Sicily. I never use green ones because I find them too bitter—they are just unripe red peppers and you need all that Mediterranean sunshine and sweetness trapped inside the red and yellow ones. When cooked, the peppers should be very soft indeed and well caramelized for this recipe to be properly successful. Delicious on its own, this dish will also make a fantastic partner to a grilled steak.

sautéed bell peppers with olives and capers

peperoni alla siciliana

⅓ cup extra virgin olive oil

2 medium red bell peppers, halved, seeded, and cut into thin strips

2 medium yellow bell peppers, halved, seeded, and cut into thin strips

4 garlic cloves, thinly sliced

6 anchovy fillets in oil

3 tablespoons wine vinegar

2 tablespoons salted capers, rinsed and soaked in water for 10 minutes, then drained

½ cup mixed whole black and green olives

sea salt and freshly ground black pepper

Serves 4

Heat the oil in a large skillet. Add the bell peppers and garlic cloves and cook over fairly high heat for 10 minutes, stirring often to prevent burning, until they start to caramelize. Alternatively, you can do this all in a roasting pan in a hot oven, roasting them at 425°F for about 20 minutes, turning once. However, I would keep the garlic cloves whole in this case to prevent them burning.

When well caramelized, stir in the anchovies and cook, stirring for about 2 minutes until they dissolve. Add the vinegar and stir-fry for a few minutes to let the flavors develop and the vinegar evaporate. Finally, stir in the capers and olives and continue to cook for a couple of minutes until heated through. Add salt and pepper to taste, then serve hot or at room temperature.

The saltiness of pancetta or bacon is the perfect partner for zucchini, which are sweet, though they can be a little mild. The mixture of pancetta and thyme really brings out their flavor, as long as you cook it all over high heat to concentrate the juices and stop the zucchini becoming too wet.

zucchini sautéed with pancetta and thyme

zucchine saltate con pancetta e timo

1 lb. zucchini

3 tablespoons olive oil

½ cup cubetti di pancetta (cubed Italian bacon or prosciutto) or lardons

1 tablespoon chopped fresh thyme

sea salt (optional) and freshly ground black pepper

freshly squeezed juice of ½ lemon

Serves 4

Trim the zucchini and cut into cubes. Heat the oil in a skillet, add the pancetta, and sauté until golden. Add the zucchini and sauté over brisk heat for 3–4 minutes, tossing them around the pan from time to time until the cut sides start to turn golden.

When golden, add the thyme and plenty of black pepper (you probably won't need any salt). Season with a squeeze of lemon juice and serve immediately.

squash

My favorite way with zucchini! It changes their watery blandness into sweet and crunchy mouthfuls with just a hint of mint. Salting the zucchini before adding them to the batter draws out the water, concentrating the flavor. The batter is light and, if fried at the correct temperature, it doesn't absorb any oil at all.

zucchini and mint fritters
frittelle di zucchini e menta

1¼ lb. zucchini

finely grated zest of 1 unwaxed lemon

2 tablespoons chopped fresh mint

oil, for cooking

sea salt and freshly ground black pepper

lemon wedges, to serve

batter

2 eggs, separated

2 tablespoons olive oil

1 cup lager-style beer

1 cup all-purpose flour

sea salt and freshly ground black pepper

an electric deep-fryer (optional)

Serves 4

To make the batter, put the egg yolks in a bowl, beat well, then slowly beat in the oil, followed by the beer, then the flour. Season with salt and pepper to taste. Cover and let rest for 1 hour.

Meanwhile, grate the zucchini coarsely, toss with salt, put in a strainer, and let drain for 10 minutes. Rinse well, then pat dry with paper towels. Put them in a bowl, add the lemon zest, mint, salt, and pepper, and stir well.

Just before cooking, put the egg whites, salt, and pepper in a bowl and beat until firm. Gently fold into the batter. Heat the oil to 375°F in a deep-fryer or saucepan with frying basket. Mix the grated zucchini with enough batter to bind them.

Working in batches, slide about 6 small spoonfuls at a time into the hot oil and fry for 2–3 minutes until golden and crisp. Drain the fritters on paper towels, sprinkle with salt, and serve hot with lemon wedges.

This dish proves the motto is "keep it simple." I use a good firm squash like butternut or kabocha squash, or pumpkin, for this—the wetter, more spongy ones don't work as well. The big, brown-skinned pumpkins sold in Italy and France are the best though, because you can cut them into good, thick slices.

sautéed pumpkin with rosemary and balsamic

zucca in padella con rosmarino e aceto balsamico

1 lb. firm-fleshed squash or pumpkin

3 tablespoons olive oil

2 tablespoons brown sugar

¼ cup balsamic vinegar

2 sprigs of rosemary

1 tablespoon chopped fresh rosemary

sea salt and freshly ground black pepper

Serves 4

Cut the pumpkin into thick slices, cut off the outer skin, and scrape out any seeds. Heat the olive oil in a large skillet and add the pumpkin. Sauté for about 5 minutes on each side until golden brown and tender. If not cooked by then, add about 1 cup water to the pan and cover with a lid. Cook for another 5 minutes until tender. Remove the pumpkin to a serving dish and keep it warm, reserving the juices in the pan.

Add the sugar, balsamic vinegar, and the sprigs of rosemary to the pan and bring to a boil. Boil hard until the liquid has been reduced to about 3 tablespoons. Stir in the chopped rosemary. Trickle the liquid over the pumpkin and season with salt and pepper. Serve immediately.

index

conversion chart

Weights and measures have been rounded up
or down slightly to make measuring easier.

Volume equivalents:

American	Metric	Imperial
1 teaspoon	5 ml	
1 tablespoon	15 ml	
¼ cup	60 ml	2 fl.oz.
⅓ cup	75 ml	2½ fl.oz.
½ cup	125 ml	4 fl.oz.
⅔ cup	150 ml	5 fl.oz. (¼ pint)
¾ cup	175 ml	6 fl.oz.
1 cup	250 ml	8 fl.oz.

Weight equivalents: **Measurements:**

Imperial	Metric	Inches	cm
1 oz.	25 g	¼ inch	5 mm
2 oz.	50 g	½ inch	1 cm
3 oz.	75 g	¾ inch	1.5 cm
4 oz.	125 g	1 inch	2.5 cm
5 oz.	150 g	2 inches	5 cm
6 oz.	175 g	3 inches	7 cm
7 oz.	200 g	4 inches	10 cm
8 oz. (½ lb.)	250 g	5 inches	12 cm
9 oz.	275 g	6 inches	15 cm
10 oz.	300 g	7 inches	18 cm
11 oz.	325 g	8 inches	20 cm
12 oz.	375 g	9 inches	23 cm
13 oz.	400 g	10 inches	25 cm
14 oz.	425 g	11 inches	28 cm
15 oz.	475 g	12 inches	30 cm
16 oz. (1 lb.)	500 g		
2 lb.	1 kg		

Oven temperatures:

110°C	(225°F)	Gas ¼
120°C	(250°F)	Gas ½
140°C	(275°F)	Gas 1
150°C	(300°F)	Gas 2
160°C	(325°F)	Gas 3
180°C	(350°F)	Gas 4
190°C	(375°F)	Gas 5
200°C	(400°F)	Gas 6
220°C	(425°F)	Gas 7
230°C	(450°F)	Gas 8
240°C	(475°F)	Gas 9